SOLO PIANO

Brazilian BOSSA NOVAS for Piano

Music Minus One

16011

Music Minus One

16011

CONTENTS

ISBN 978-1-59615-822-1

SUGGESTIONS FOR USING THIS MMO EDITION

We have tried to create a product that will provide you an easy way to learn and perform these compositions with a full ensemble in the comfort of your own home. The following MMO features and techniques will help you maximize the effectiveness of the MMO practice and performance system:

Because it involves a fixed accompaniment performance, there is an inherent lack of flexibility in tempo. We have observed generally accepted tempi, and always in the originally intended key, but some may wish to perform at a different tempo, or to slow down or speed up the accompaniment for practice purposes; or to alter the piece to a more comfortable key. You can purchase from MMO specialized CD players & recorders which allow variable speed while maintaining proper pitch, and vice versa. This is an indispensable tool for the serious musician and you may wish to look into purchasing this useful piece of equipment for full enjoyment of all your MMO editions.

We want to provide you with the most useful practice and performance accompaniments possible. If you have any suggestions for improving the MMO system, please feel free to contact us. You can reach us by e-mail at *info@musicminusone.com.*

Blue Bossa

This is a bossa nova with a decided jazz flavor. There is plenty of room for the piano to stretch out here, and it seizes the opportunity after playing melody in the first chorus. The ensuing improvisation quickly takes on a strong authoritative percussiveness and continues in that vein right to the end. The four-bar exchanges between piano and drum solos add excitement and good fun to the playing. J.O.

Music by Kenny Dorham

21 Cm Fm7 Edim Fm7

25 Dm7♭5 G7 Cm7/E♭ Ddim Cm7

29 E♭m7 A♭7 D♭

33 Dm7♭5 G+7 Cm6

37 Cm Fm7

41 Dm7♭5 G7 Cm7

45 E♭m7 A♭7 D♭

RH

49
Dm7♭5
G7
Cm
2
2
3
53
Cm
Fm7
57
Dm7♭5
G+7
Cm6
61
E♭m7
A♭7♭9
D♭maj7
65
Dm7♭5
G7
Cm
Dm7♭5
G7
3
3
69
Cm
Fm7

73
Dm7♭5
G13
Cm7
77
E♭m7
A♭7
D♭maj7
D♭6
81
Dm7♭5
3
G+7
Cm6
85
Cm
Fm7
89
Dm7♭5
G+7
Cm6
93
E♭m7
A♭9
D♭

97
Dm7b5
G7
Cm
Dm7b5
G7
RH
101
Cm
Fm7
105
Dm7b5
DRUM SOLO
2
2
Ebm7
Ab7
Dbmaj7
Db
109
113
Dm7b5
DRUM SOLO
2
2
117
Cm7
Fm7

121
4
DRUM SOLO
4
125
E♭m7
A♭7
D♭
129
Dm7♭5
3
DRUM SOLO
3
133
Cm
G♭7
Fm7
Edim
Fm7
137
Dm7♭5
G7
Cm
Bdim
Cm
141
E♭m7
A♭7
D♭
Dm7♭5
G7
Cm7
145
3
3

149
Cm
Fm7
Edim
Fm7
153
Dm7b5
G7
Cm7
Bdim
Cm
157
Ebm7
Ab7
Dbmaj7
161
Dm7b5
G7
3
Cm
165
Dm7b5
G+7
Cm6
169
Dm7b5
G+7#9
f
Cm7

The Girl From Impanema

The intro establishes the bossa nova feel with guitar, trombone and rhythm section. This very attactive Latin rhythm traditionally has the piano playing single note figures much of the time. I chose to stay with this established mode simply because it seemed best. A few well-placed left hand chords help to add spice and rhythmic interest. The playing remains stylistically consistent, simple and uncomplicated to the end. J.O.

Words and Music by Vinicius De Moraes and
Antonio Carlos Jobim

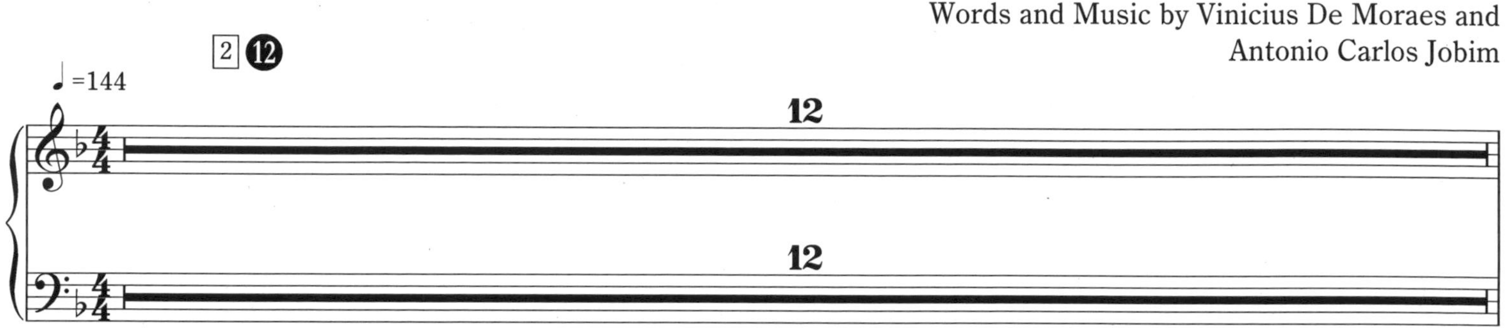

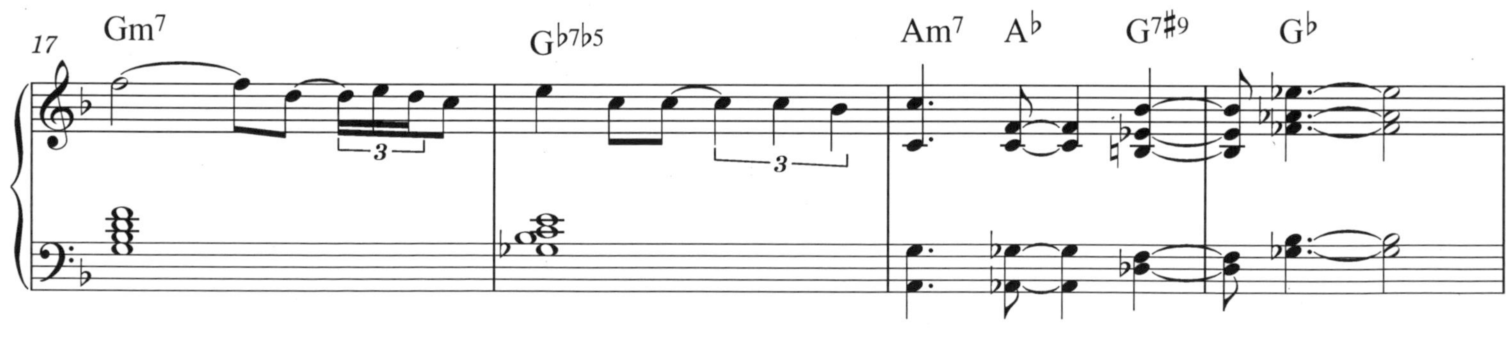

25
Gm7
3
C
Fmaj9
3
3
3
3
29
G♭maj7
B7
33
F♯m7
3
D7
37
Gm7
RH
40
Am7
D7♭5
Gm7
C7♭5
3
3
3
3
45
Fmaj7
G9

49 Gm7 C Fmaj9

52 C7♭9 F G9

57 Gm7 G♭7 NC

61 F69 G

65 Gm7 G♭7 Fmaj9

69 G♭maj7♭5 B7

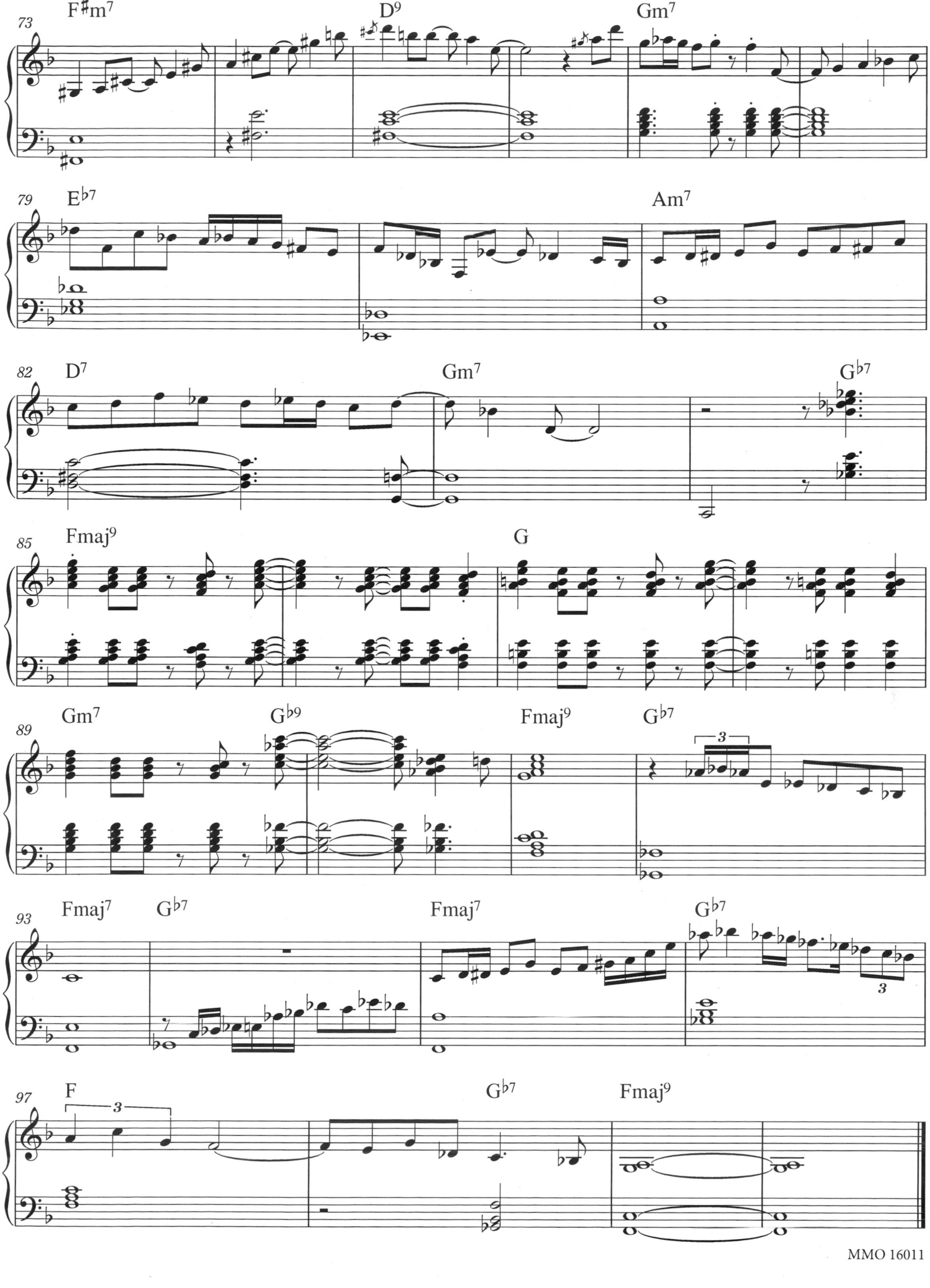

73 F♯m7 D9 Gm7

79 E♭7 Am7

82 D7 Gm7 G♭7

85 Fmaj9 G

89 Gm7 G♭9 Fmaj9 G♭7

93 Fmaj7 G♭7 Fmaj7 G♭7

97 F G♭7 Fmaj9

No More Blues

I really enjoyed putting this track together from scratch since No More Blues is a beautifully constructed Latin piece that is ideal for improvisation. It is simply sheer fun to perform. After playing melody through the entire first chorus, the improvisation starts at the pickup into bar 77. Notice how the change from the key of F minor to F major imparts a happy uplifting boost in the music that actually inspires the player to ride the crest of the exalted mood it creates. I'm sure that you will enjoy this piece as much as I do. J.O.

Music by Antonio Carlos Jobim
English words by Jon Hendricks and Jessie Cavanaugh
Original Words by Vinicius DeMoraes

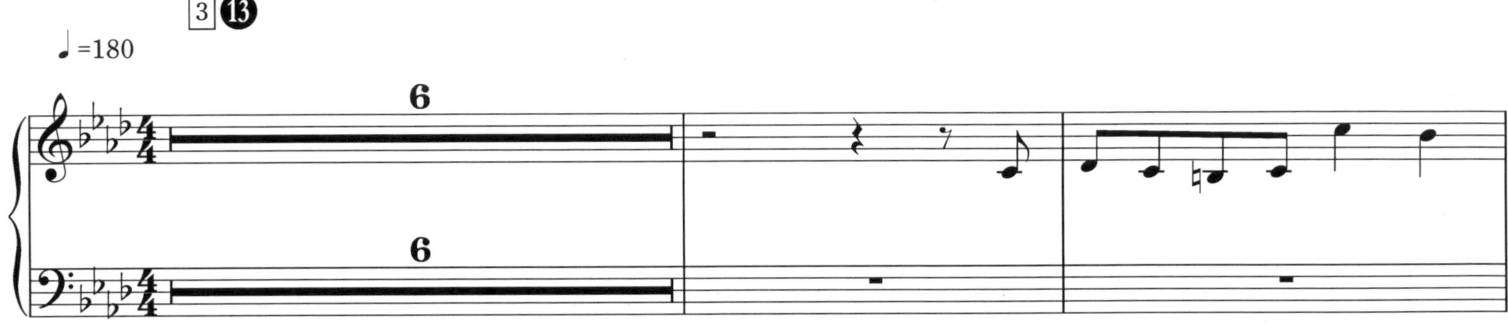

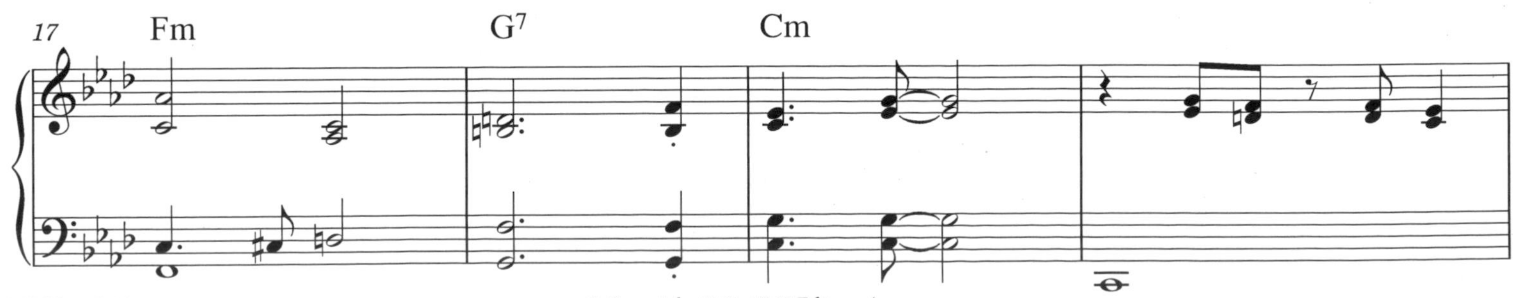

21 Bb m7 C7 3
25 Fm Ab7 G7 Dm7 G7
29 C7b9 Fm7 F7b9
33 Bb m7 Db9 C9 Fm7 Fm6
37 G7 C7b9 Fm Bb m Fm
41 F7 E7 Eb7 D7 Gm7

45
Gm7
C7
Bdim
F
3
49
F/A
A♭dim
Gm7
C7
53
Dm7
G7
Gm7
C7
57
F
G7
61
A7
A7♭9
Dm7
D♭dim
Cm6
F7
3
65
B♭maj7
E♭11
Am7
D11
D7

69
Gm7 D♭7 C7 B♭7 A7 E♭7 D7
73
G7 F
77
Fm G7 Dm7♭5 G7 D♭7
81
C7 Fm Gm7 C7
85
Fm A♭7 G7 Cm B7
89
B♭m7 C7 C7
3

93
Fm
Fm6
G13
G7
D♭9
97
C7
C7
Fm7
B♭m7
D♭maj7
C7
C13
Fm6
Fm6
101
G7♭9
C7
Fm
105
F
E7
E♭7
D7
G7
109
Gm7
C7
Fm
B♭7
113
3

117
Am7
Am7
A♭dim
Gm7
D♭7
C7
121
G7
Gm7
D♭9
C7
125
F
G7
Dm7
G7
129
A7♭9
Dm7
D♭dim
Cm6
F7
133
B♭maj7
E♭11
Am7
D11
D7
137
D♭7
C7
B♭7
A7
E♭7
D7

141
G7
C11
Am7
E♭7
D7
D+7

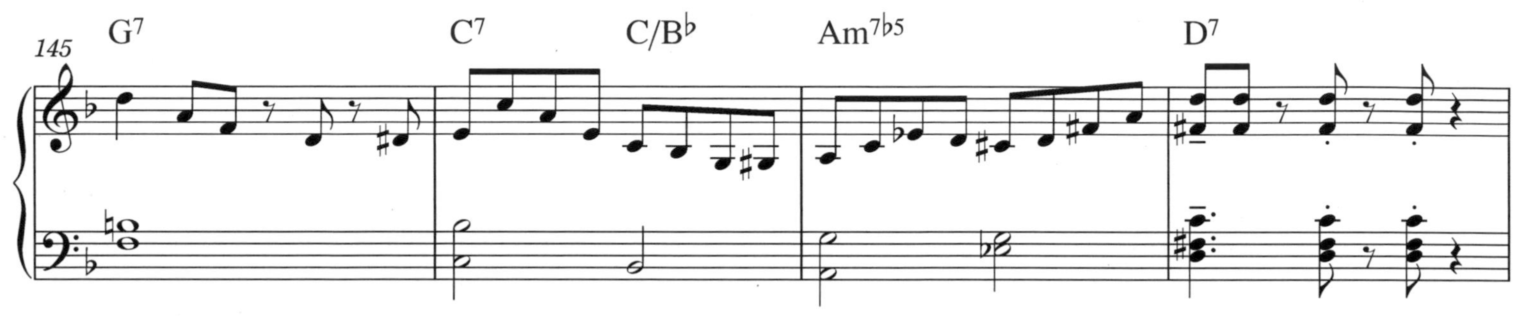
145
G7
C7
C/B♭
Am7♭5
D7

149
G7
C11
F

Triste

After a repeating bossa nova guitar figure supports an overlay of woodwinds, piano enters at the chorus with melody in sixths, and then changes to various textures for contrast. It next plays around the melody with idiomatic pianistic configurations typical of the bossa nova style. Flute and keyboard play a section with the arranger's "written improvisation" based upon the chords of the first sixteen bars of chorus. Piano then re-enters with pianistic elaborations and figurations as before and seizes the opportunity to improvise over a repeating band figure that fades out to silence. J.O.

Words and Music by Antonio Carlos Jobim

21
D♭
B♭m7
E♭m7
A♭9
C♯m7
F♯7
Bm7
E7
25
A
Am7
7
29
A
3
Em7
33
D
Dm
Dm6
A/C♯
37
Bm7
Bm7
E7♭9
Am7
8va
D9

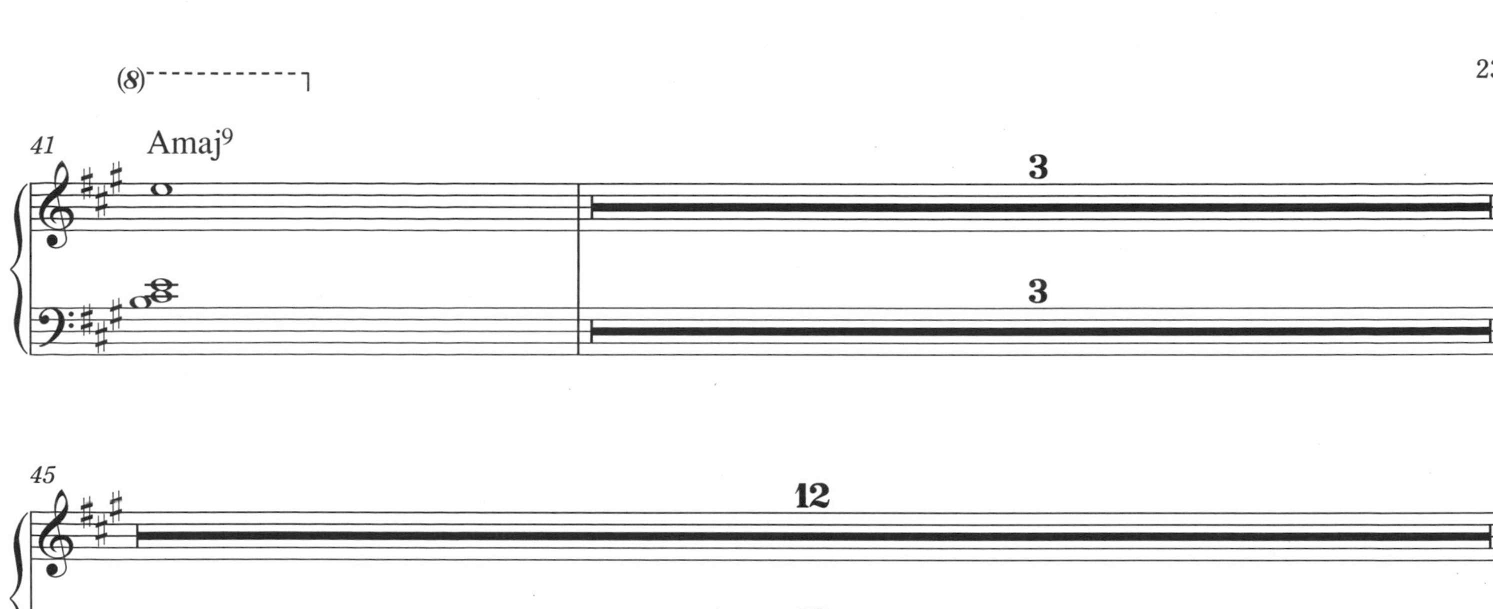
(8)
41
Amaj9
3
3

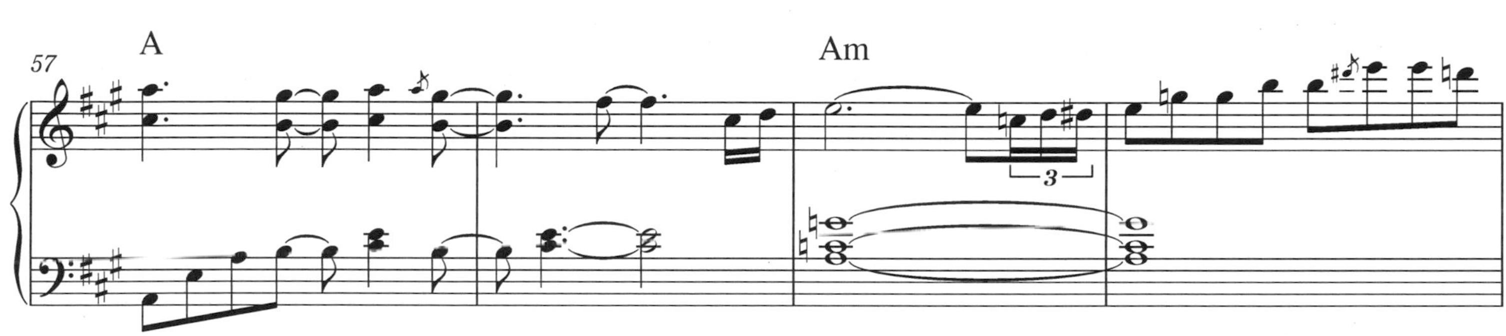
45
12
12

57
A
Am
3

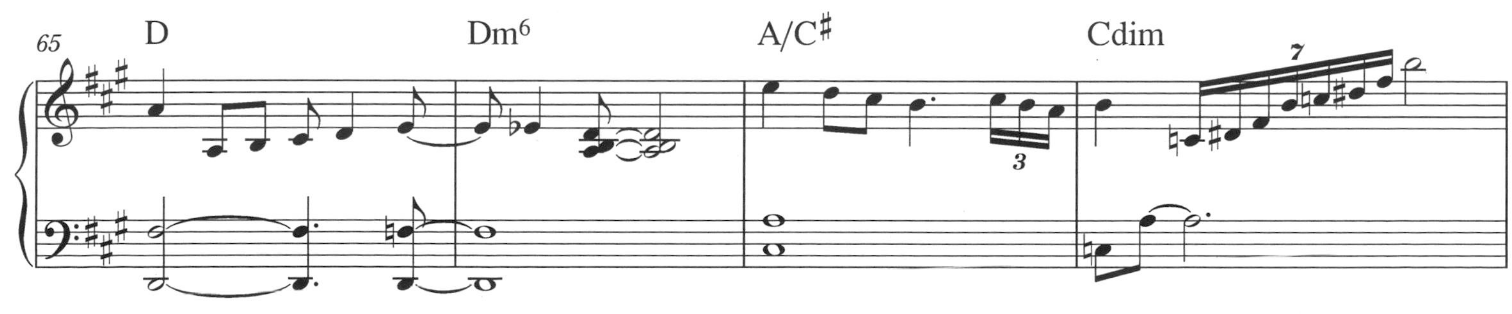
61
Amaj7
3
Em7
Em7
3
A7♭9
3

65
D
Dm6
A/C♯
3
Cdim
7
69
Bm7
Bm7
Am7
8va

(8)
D9
73
3

(8)
77

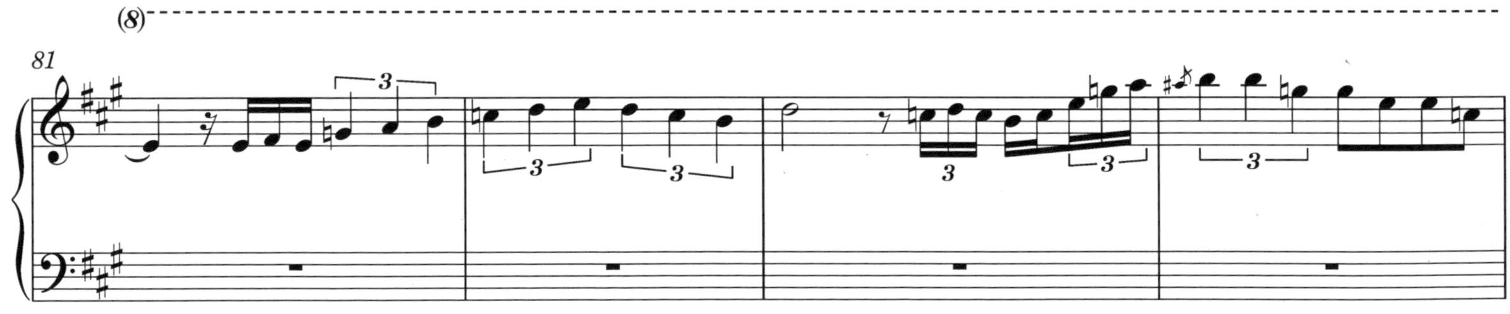
(8)
81
3

(8)
85
loco
3

Black Orpheus

The guitar sets a quiet contemplative mood for this piece in the four bar introduction. Piano follows in the next thirty-two measures with a simple playing of melody without much elaboration other than simple fills where the melody pauses. The improvisation that follows in the next section maintains the calm, unhurried pace, seeking always to create melodic continuity with phrases that flow logically one to the other. Near the end, the piano is left unaccompanied to finish the piece with an improvised cadenza-like phrase that is joined by the guitar in its final notes. J.O.

Music by Luiz Bonfa

21 Am
Bm7♭5 E7
Am
Bm7♭5 E7
25 Em7♭5
Em7♭5 A7♭9
Dm
Dm Dm/C
29 Bm7♭5
Bm7♭5 E7
Am7
F
33 Bm7♭5
E7
Am
Bm7♭5 E7
37 Am
Bm7♭5 E7
Am7
Bm7♭5 E7
41 Am
Dm7 G7
C
C♯dim

45
Dm7
G7
C
Fmaj7
49
Bm7♭5
E7
Am
Bm7♭5
E7
53
Am
E7
Am
E11
E7
57
Em7♭5
A7
Dm
RH
61
E7
Am
Am/G
Fmaj7
65
Bm7♭5
E7
E7♭9
Am

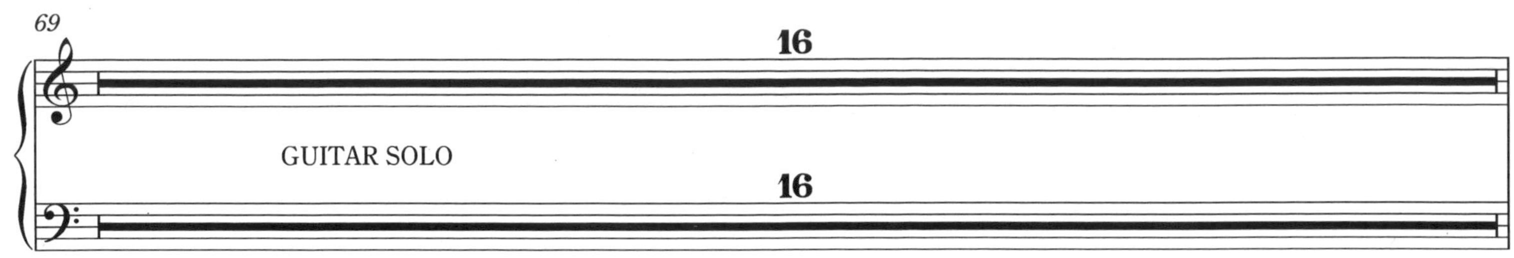
69
16
GUITAR SOLO
16

Am
Bm7♭5
E7
Bm7♭5
E7
85

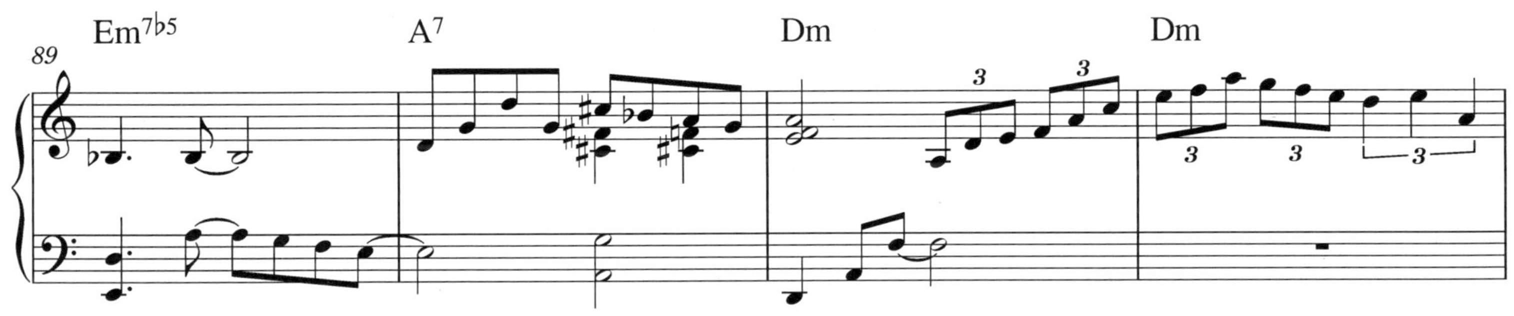
Em7♭5
A7
Dm
Dm
89
3
3
3
3
3

Dm
Bm7♭5
E7
Am7
Am7/G
F
93
3

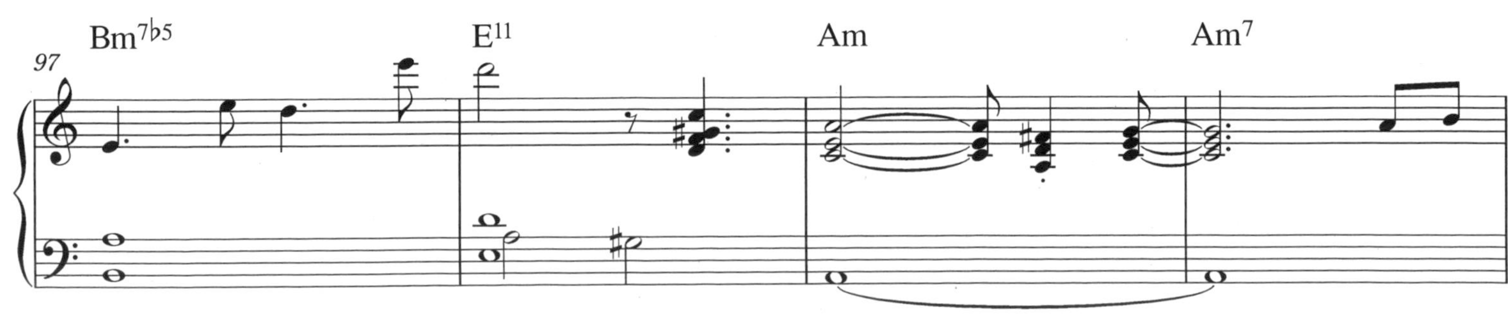
Bm7♭5
E11
Am
Am7
97

Dm7
Am7
Dm7
Am7
Dm7
Em7
Am
101

Dm7
Am
Dm7
Am
Dm7
Em7
Am
105

Dm7
E♭dim
C/E
F
F♯m7♭5
E7
Am
109
slowly with track
freely

Am
113
slower
very slowly

Meditation

The intro features a sultry flute against the bossa nova beat. The piano continues the feel with single note melody sprinkled with an occasional punctuating LH chord (an established trademark in this style). As a general rule, it is a good idea to stay within the traditional parameters of any given style. Always seek, though, to vary textures in order to sustain interest and avoid boredom. Notice how, in the second phrase, I made use of somewhat fuller voicings for contrast. The rest of this piece reflects continued adherence to the notion of achieving contrast through textural variation. J.O.

Words and Music by Antonio Carlos Jobim and Mendonca
English lyric by Norman Gilbert

B♭
B♭maj7
Dm7
G+7
Cm7
A♭13
E♭m7
A♭7
Dm7
G+7
Cm7
F9
E♭69
A♭13
Dm7
D♭dim
Cm7
F+7
B♭maj7
A7
A+7

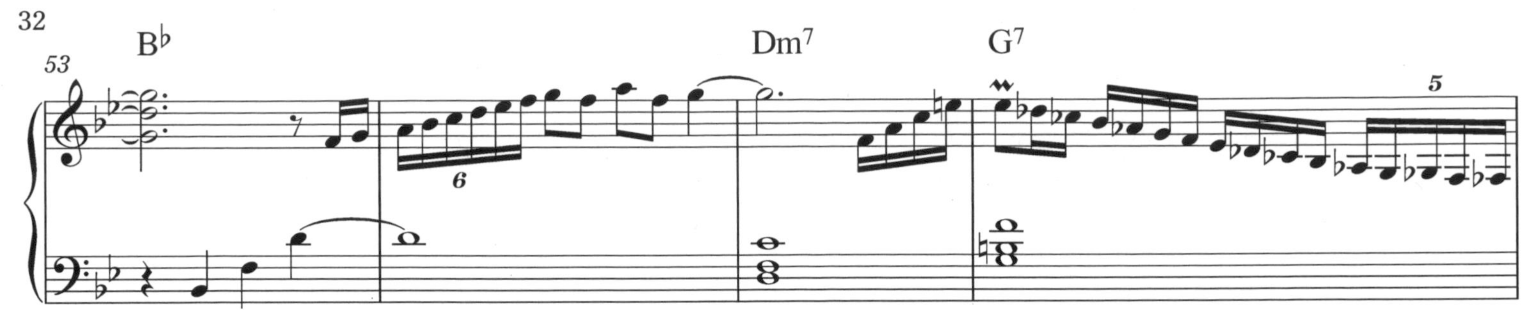
53
B♭
Dm7
G7
6
5

57
Cm7
3
3
5
A♭9

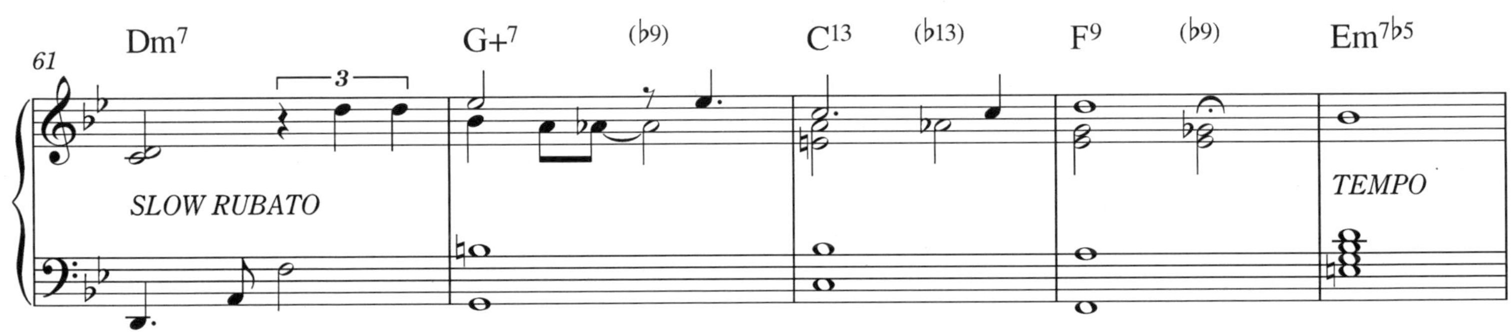
61
Dm7
3
SLOW RUBATO
G+7
(♭9)
C13
(♭13)
F9
(♭9)
Em7♭5
TEMPO

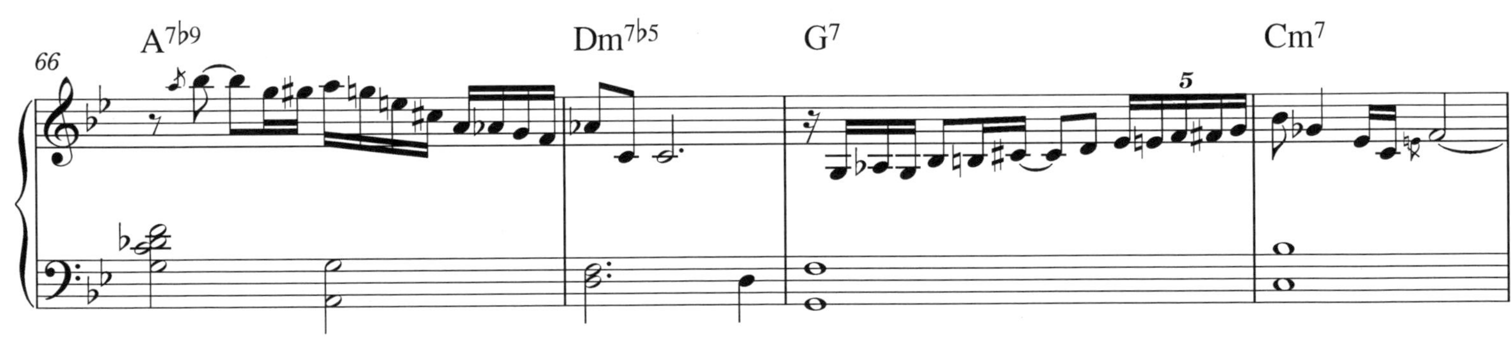
66
A7♭9
Dm7♭5
G7
5
Cm7

70
F7
B♭maj7
F+7
rit.

Someone To Light Up My Life

This is one of the most beautiful Latin melodies ever written. Its harmonic construction is a model of excellence and naturalness. One chord follows the other in a logical sequence that can perhaps be best described as inevitable. It is this natural flow in the harmony that makes improvisation seem so natural and easy. You'll see what I mean as you play through this lovely piece. J.O.

Written by De Moraes, Jobim, Lees

21
B♭
Am7♭5
D7
Gm7
G♭dim
RH
E♭
Dm7♭5
G+7
27
E♭
E♭
Em7♭5
E♭m7
B♭/D
32
D♭9
C7
F11
B♭
Cm7
F7
37
B♭
Am7♭5
D7
Gm7
F♯m7
Fm7
B♭7
41
E♭
Dm7♭5
G+7
Cm7
Cm7

45
F7
F7
F
B♭
Cm7
C♯dim
B♭/D
Em7♭5
mp
f
mf
mp
f
mf

50
A+7♭9
Dm7
G7♭9
Cm7
F7
5

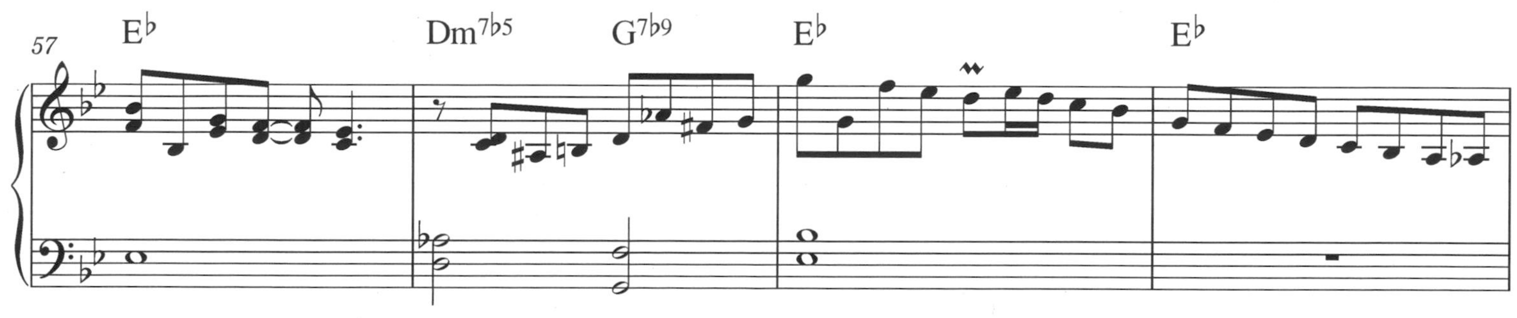
53
B♭
Am7♭5
D9
Gm7
G♭7
Fm7
B♭

57
E♭
Dm7♭5
G7♭9
E♭
E♭
61
Em7♭5
E♭m7
B♭/D
D♭9

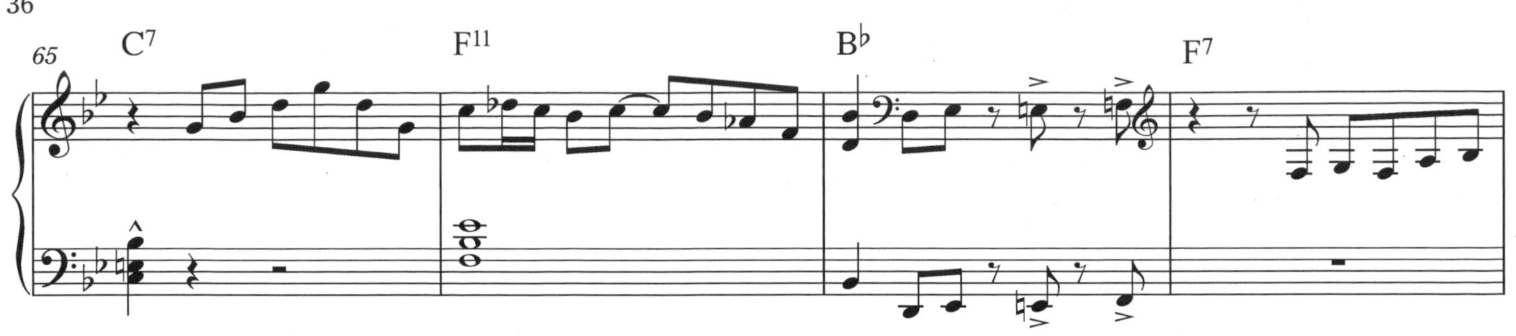
65
C7
F11
B♭
F7

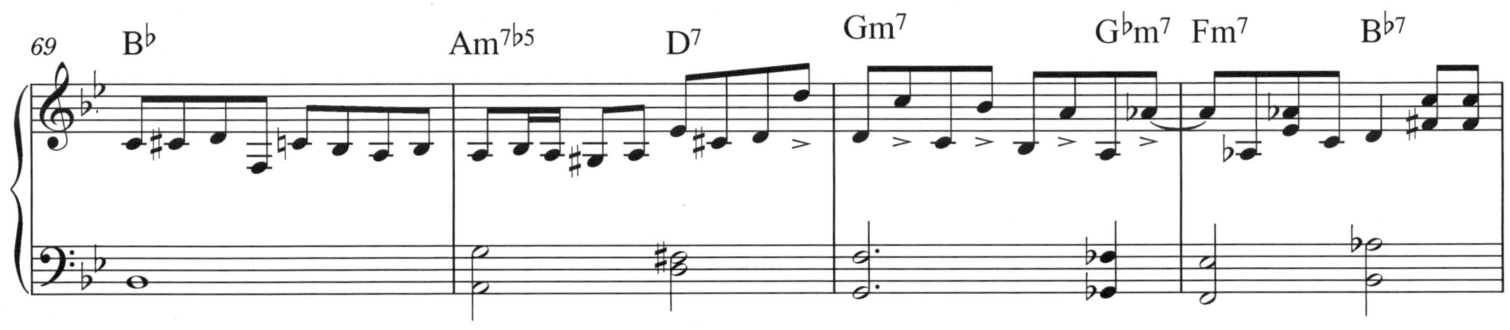
69
B♭
Am7♭5
D7
Gm7
G♭m7
Fm7
B♭7

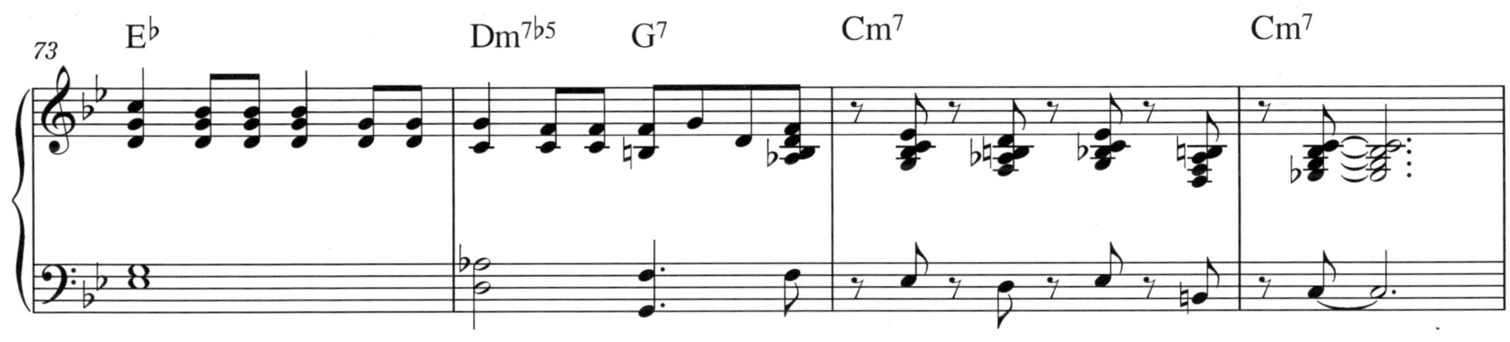
73
E♭
Dm7♭5
G7
Cm7
Cm7

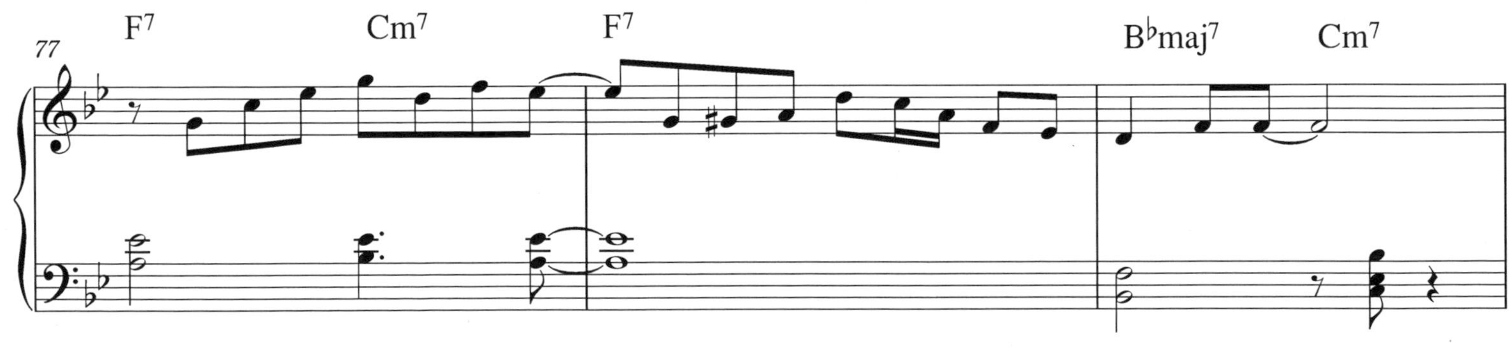
77
F7
Cm7
F7
B♭maj7
Cm7

80
C♯dim
Dm7
Em7
3
A7

83
Dm7
G+7
Cm7
F11
B♭
Am7♭5
D7
87
Gm7
G♭dim
Fm7
B♭7
RH
E♭
Dm7♭5
G+7
E♭
92
E♭
Em7♭5
E♭m7
B♭/D
96
D♭9
C7
F11
99
B♭
A♭9
B♭
A♭9
103
Gm7
G♭9
F11
F7♭9
B♭
mf

Quiet Nights Of Quiet Stars

Flute and strings with rhythm section immediately establish a light bossa nova beat during the intro. Piano starts the chorus with single-note melody supported by LH chords. This voicing has become such a traditional part of the piano's role in bossa nova as to make it virtually obligatory. The next phrase features improvisation that preserves the essential contours of melody. Varied textures, including block chords are used here. Note how the piano accepts the invitation to improvise over a repeating flute and string figure at the end of this arrangement. J.O.

Antonio Carlos Jobim
English lyric by Gene Lees

8va
loco
28
D7/A
G♯dim
32
Gm7
C11
C+7
F
36
Fm7
B♭13
Em7
Am7
40
Dm7
G11
G7/F
Em7
A7♭5
8va
44
Dm7
G13
loco
G7♭13
Cm7
7
7

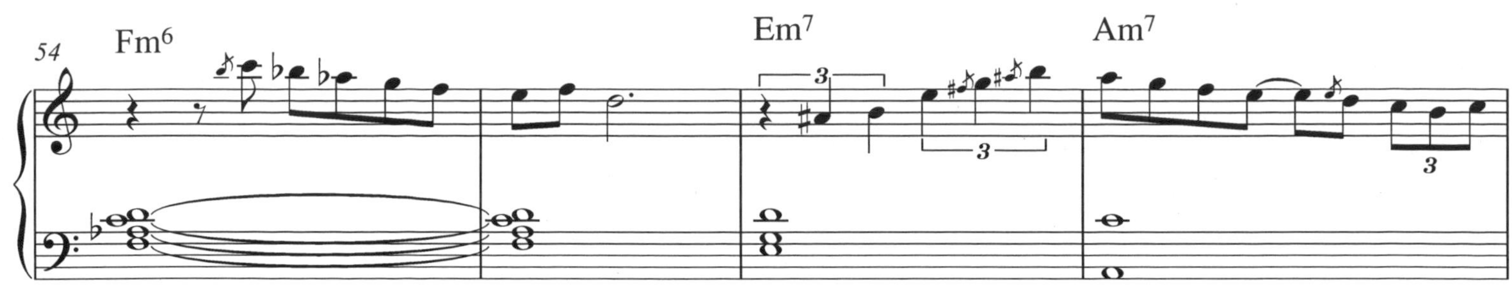
54
Fm6
Em7
Am7
3
3
3

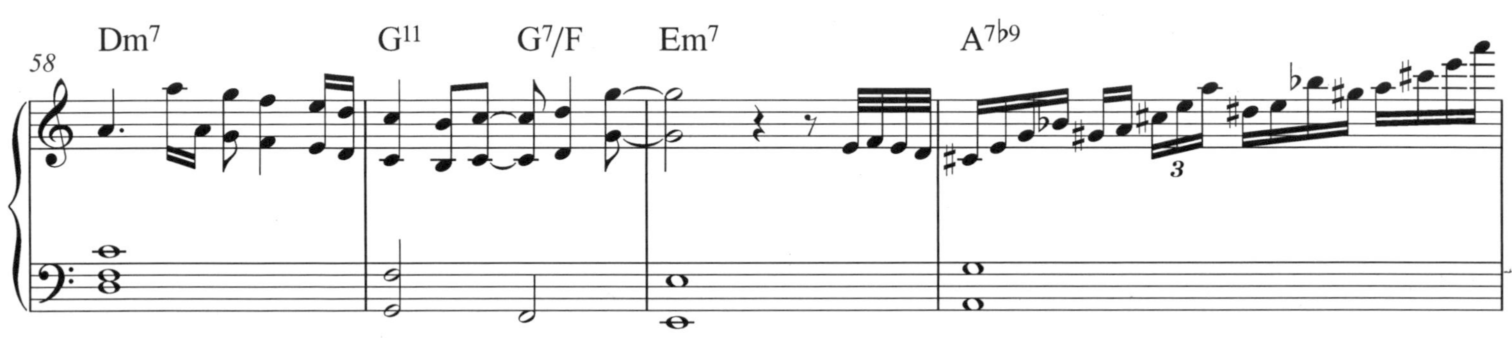
58
Dm7
G11
G7/F
Em7
A7♭9
3

62
Dm7
Dm7
G7♭9
Cm7

66
B♭m7
Cm
3
7
6

70
B♭m7
Cm

Once I Loved

This is yet another example of the melodic and harmonic genius of Antonio Carlos Jobim. In addition to the melodic beauty of this piece, notice the inevitable logical progression of chords that have become his trademark. This feature is of great significance to the improviser since what he is doing can be accurately described as "carving new melodies out of existing harmonies." It follows that the more logically these chords progress, the more enjoyable it is for the player to easily weave in and out ot them as he plays. J.O.

Music by Antonio Carlos Jobim
English Words by Ray Gilbert
Original Words by Vinicius DeMoraes

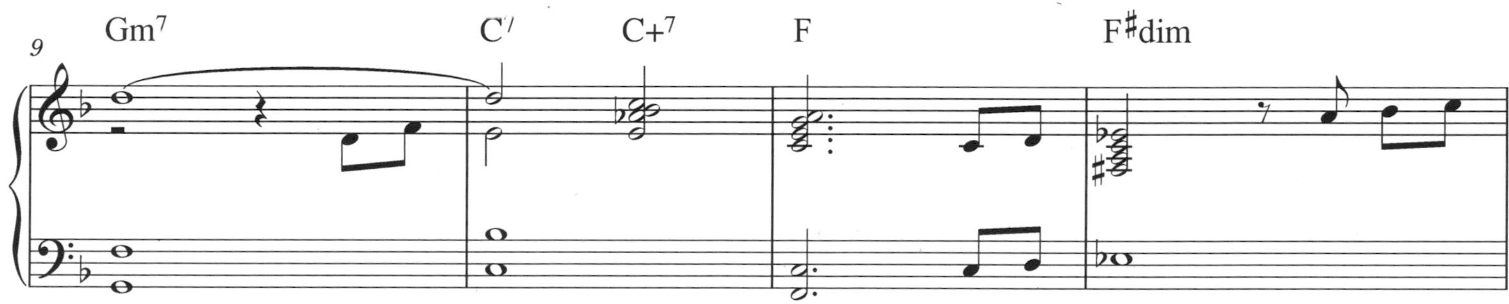

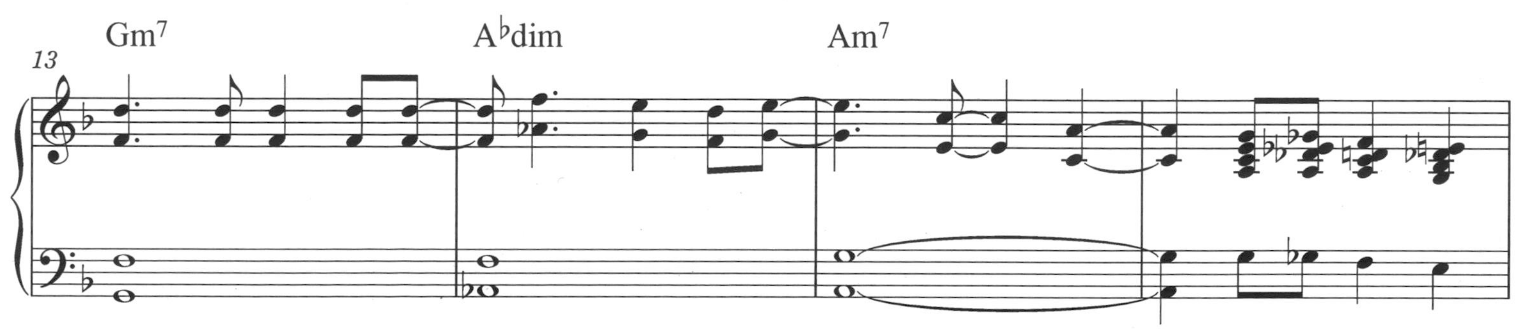

21
Em7♭5
3
3
A7
3
D
D7♭9
25
Gm7
3
3
3
C13
C7♭13
F
F♯dim
29
Gm7
A♭dim
Am7
RH
33
Fm7
B♭
E♭
3
3
E♭
37
Em7♭5
3
A7
D
G7
3
Cmaj7
G♭7
F7
B7
43
B♭maj7
Bm7♭5
3
3
B♭m6
D7/A
A♭dim

49
Gm7
A7
Dm
Gm7
54
C13
C7♭13
F69
F♯dim
Gm7
58
G♯dim
F/A
Fm7
B♭7
63
E♭
E♭6
RH
Em7♭5
B♭7
E♭9
67
D9
E♭9
D7♭9
Gm7
C7

71
C♯dim
Dm7
F♯dim
Gm7
G♯dim

75
Am7
F
Fm7
B♭7

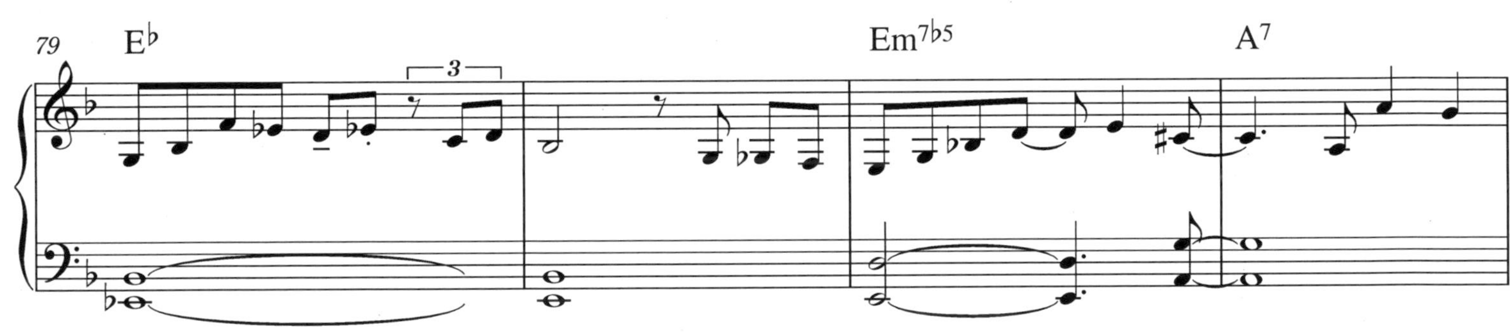
79
E♭
Em7♭5
A7

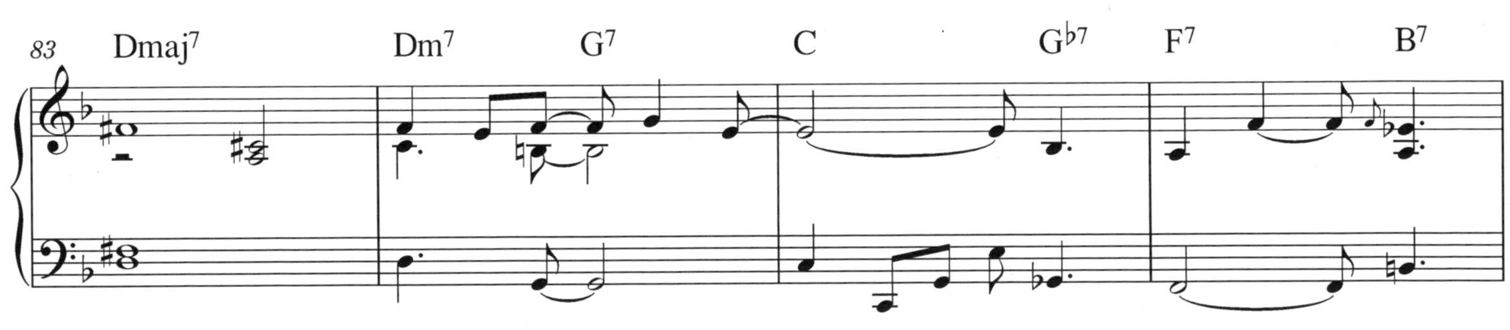
83
Dmaj7
Dm7
G7
C
G♭7
F7
B7

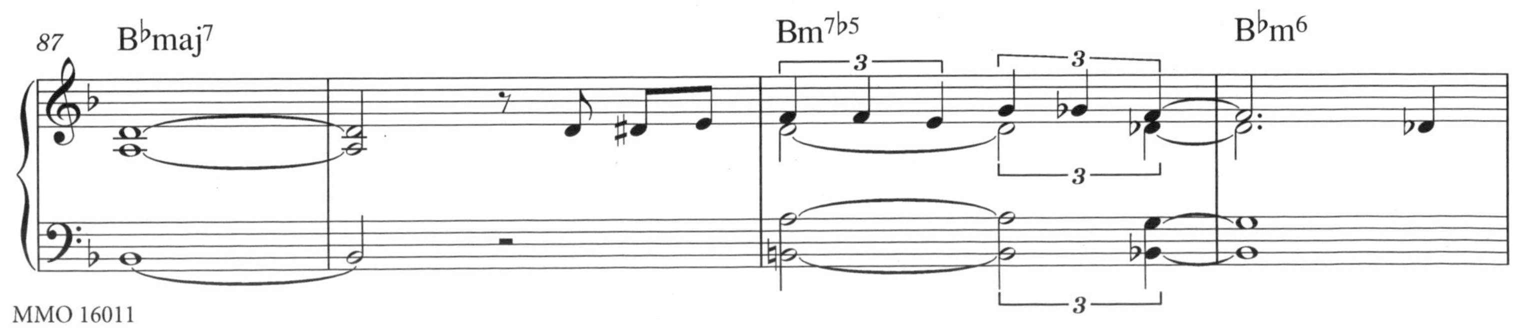
87
B♭maj7
Bm7♭5
B♭m6

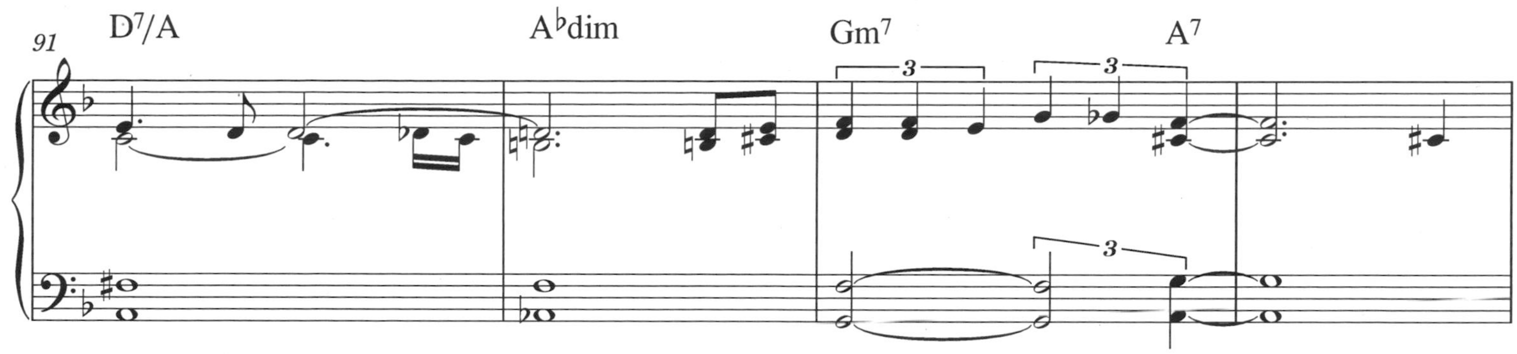
91
D7/A
A♭dim
Gm7
A7
3
3
3

95
Dm
Gm7
A7♭9
3
3
3

99
Dm/C
Bm7♭5
B♭7
A7
3

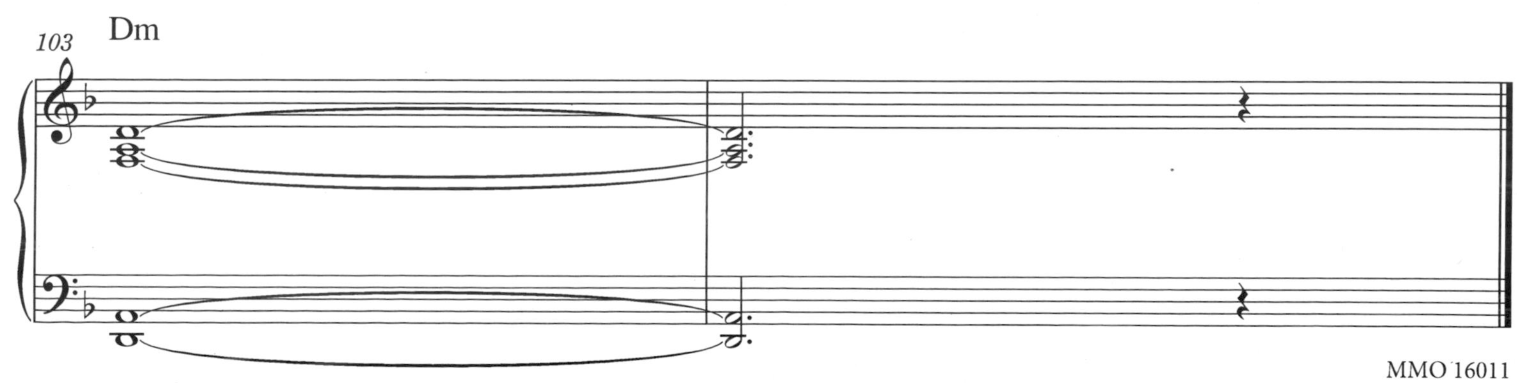
103
Dm

Wave

Guitar. flute and drums start things off and piano begins the chorus with contrasting melodic textures. The second twelve bar phrase features block chords and elaborated melody. At the bridge, I make use of melody played in a two-octave spread, followed by a single-note melody supported by left hand chords. Listen to the background track and try to understand my reasons for doing it this way. Then, as a useful exercise, do it according to your own instincts. The rest of this piece features free improvisation, a return to elaborated melody, improvisation around melody, and stronger voicings with fill-ins to herald the impending concluding section where the piano imitates a band figure and then proceeds to improvise until the music fades out. J.O.

Words and Music by Antonio Carlos Jobim

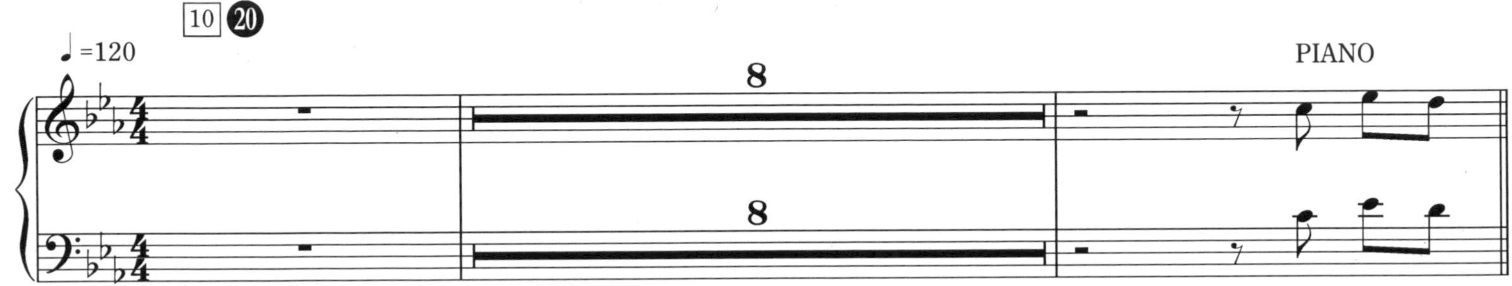

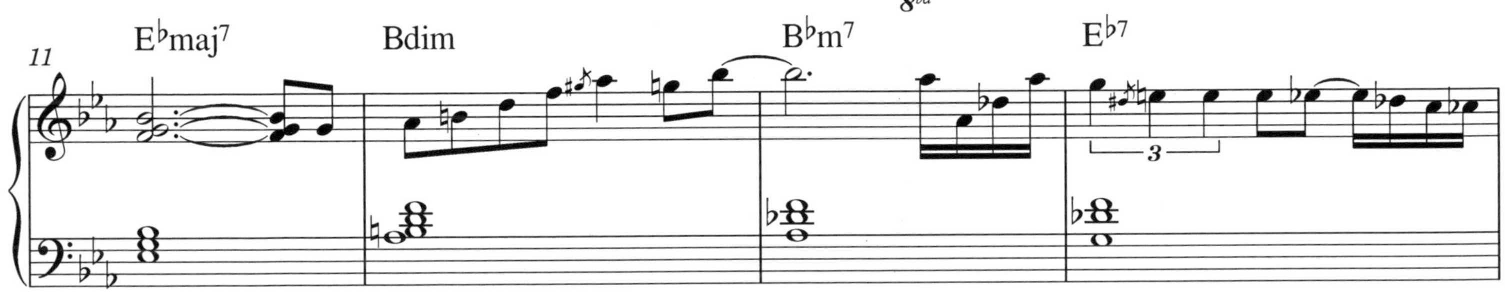

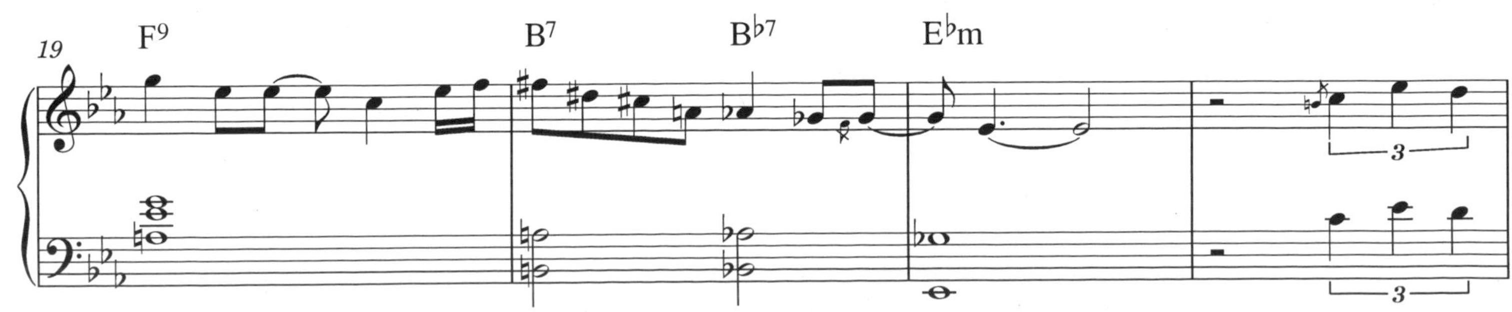

E♭maj7
Bdim
B♭m7
E♭7
A♭maj7
D♭9
G13
8va
(♭13)
C9
loco
F9
B7
B♭7
E♭m
A♭m7
D♭7
G♭
G♭maj7
F♯m7
B7
Emaj7
E♭maj7
Bdim
B♭m7
E♭7

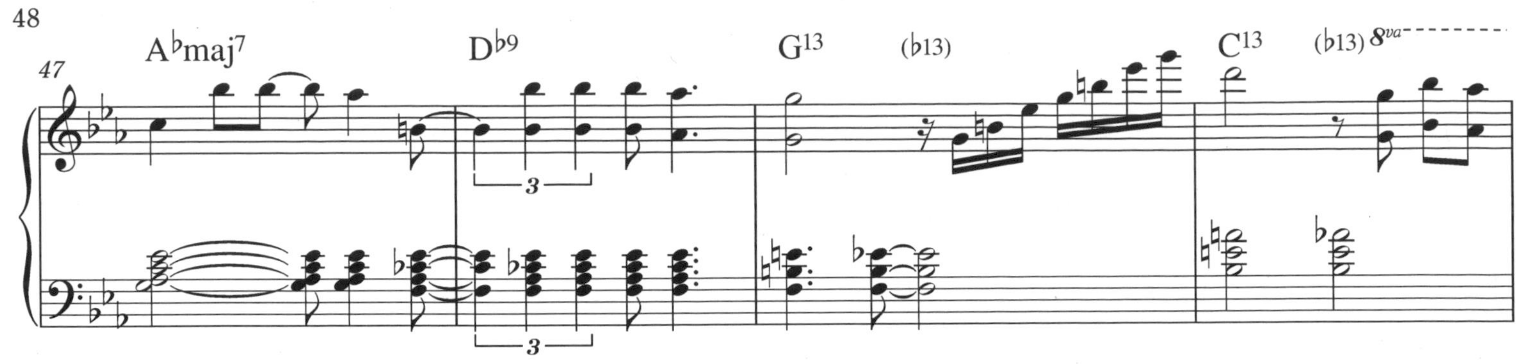

A♭maj7
D♭9
G13
(♭13)
C13
(♭13)
8va

(8)
F9
B7
B♭7
E♭m

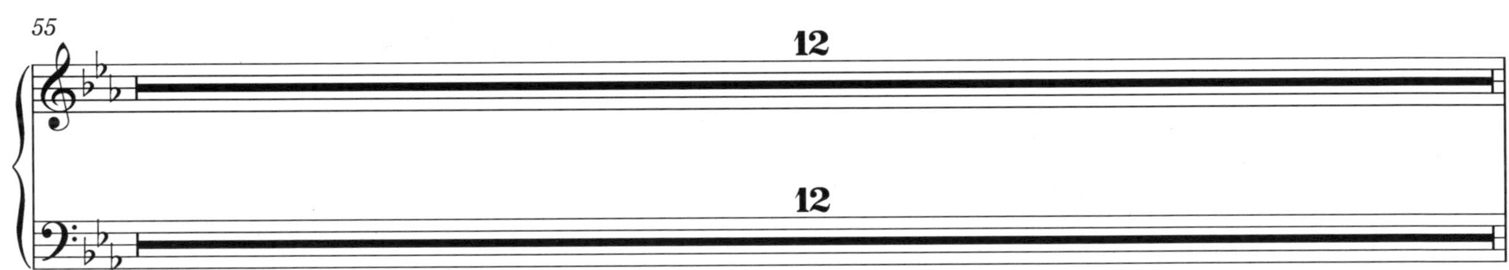

12
12

A♭m7
D♭9
G♭maj7

F♯m7
B7
Emaj7
B♭13 (♭13)
NC

E♭maj7
Bdim
B♭m7
E♭7
A♭maj7
A♭m7
G13
G+7
C9
8va
F9
B9
B♭7
loco
E♭m
NC
fade

More Pop, Blues & Jazz Classics for Piano from MUSIC MINUS ONE

2+2=5 ***A Study in Odd Times*** **..................MMO CD 2045**
Towson State College Jazz Ensemble/Hank Levy: This collection of stage band classics exploits the unusual meters which became the trademark of composer Hank Levy, whose compositions have been recorded by such greats as Stan Kenton and Don Ellis. An exciting exploration of this now-all-too-rare genre.
Bop City Revisited; Poopsie's Penthouse; A Quiet Friday; Pete Is a Four-Letter Word; Bread and Watrous; Stillness Runs Deep

Bacharach Revisited - Jack Six, arranger.MMO CD 6033
Eddie Hubbel & Lou McGarity, trombones; Harold Lieberman, trpt.; Hal McKusick, Alto Sax/clarinet; Gene Allen, baritone sax; Kenny Davern, soprano sax; Dick Wellstood, piano; Ed Shaughnessy & Jos.Cocuzzo, drums; Jack Six, Acoustic BassManny Senerchialst violin; Winston Brown2nd violin.; Karl SafranviolaRuth Linsley'cello: Here are ten of the great hits of Bacharach and David, icons of 20th-century popular music in scintillating arrangements by Jack Six and performed by one of the great pop ensembles ever put together, minus you, the piano soloist!!
Alfie; I Say a Little Prayer; Blue on Blue; Wives and Lovers (Hey, Little Girl); Walk on By; Magic Moments; Windows of the World; Do You Know the Way to San Jose?; This Guy's in Love with You; What the World Needs Now (Is Love, Sweet Love)

Blues Fusion for Piano ....MMO CD 3049
Eric Kriss, piano & electric piano - Bob Johnson, tenor and soprano sax; Stan Poplin, acoustic and electric bass; Jim Chanteloup, drums: Eight original blues compositions covering a broad range of styles from boogie-woogie to gospel to modern funk, arranged for piano, bass, drums and sax. Listen, then play along. Includes complete arrangements, suggested solo lines and performance hints for mastering blues piano styles.
Tricky Dicky; When the Spirit; Cocaine Stomp; Wailer Blues; Boogie Breakdown; Tremblin'; Yancey's Fancy; Mad Dog Blues

BOLLING Suite for Flute and Jazz Piano Trio .....MMO CD 3050
Michael Junkroski, piano - Suzanne Kirton, flute and bass flute; Kevin Mauldin, bass; Tim Miller, drums: This Suite, when first introduced, was performed by Claude Bolling and Jean-Pierre Rampal. It swiftly became the most successful chamber music recording in history with over one-half million copies purchased. Comprised of seven movements, it cleverly exploits the differences between each instrument in a wonderfully effective way. We are delighted to make it available to you, the soloist. Claude Bolling has endorsed this recording.
Suite for Flute & Jazz Piano Trio: *Baroque and Blue; Sentimentale; Javanaise; Fugace; Irlandaise; Veratile; Véloce*

From Dixie to Swing ....MMO CD 3053
Dick Wellstood, piano - 'Doc' Cheatham, trumpet; Kenny Davern, clarinet & soprano sax; Vic Dickenson, trombone; George Duvivier, bass; Gus JohnsonJr.: Jazz legends Dick Wellstood, Alphonse 'Doc' Cheatham, George Duvivier and more back you up in this amazing collection of 1950s 'Dixieland' standards in New York clubs such as Eddie Condon's and the Metropole.,minus the banjos, tubas, steamboats and magnolias! We encourage you, the soloist, to invent counter-melodies rather than mere harmony. This is a music of loose weaving parts, not one of precision ensemble figures. One of the greatest improvisational experiences any jazz player could hope to have.
Way Down Yonder in New Orleans; Red Sails in the Sunset; Second Hand Rose; Rose of Washington Square; On the Sunny Side of the Street; Exactly Like You; I Want a Little Girl; The Royal Garden Blues

Funkdawgs: Jazz Fusion Unleashed ....MMO CD 2032
Kyle Whitlock, keyboards - the Funkdawgs Band: This superb collection of jazz fusion tunes has the distinction of being a collaboration of artists across the globe, connected by virtual recording studios and modern technology. The result is great music, and you can join in the Funkdawgs ensemble using these tracks, just as each individual artist has contributed to the complete reference versions and the backing tracks. So get out your instrument and jam away!

The Isle of Orleans.......................................MMO CD 6029
Tom McDermott, piano: Native son Tim Laughlin decided he wanted to create in the style, but not necessarily using the tried and true classics, of the "Crescent City." So he assembled an extraordinary band of players, all veterans of the music, wrote a collection of new songs, and produced this extraordinary album. It won First Prize as the Best Jazz Album created in Louisiana in 2003 by Offbeat Magazine. Tim graciously made this album available to Music Minus One, remixing the music to omit the key players, clarinet, trumpet, trombone, piano, bass and drums for some of the most delectable play-alongs we offer in our catalogue. This is music rich in tradition but new to your ears. This music isn't easy but then again, to modern players, it may be, as they'll be able to negotiate the charts provided. We've provided audio samples of each song. This is music for the ages, guaranteed to pleasure players from ten to ninety. The personnel of this band is extraordinary as you can see, and the music they make together has to be experienced. Listen, can you hear that band? ***2 CD Set***
Magnolia Dance; Restless Heart; Blues for Faz; Suburban St. Parade; It's My Love Song to You; Gentilly Strut; I Know I'll See You Again; Crescent City Moon; Isle of Orleans; Monkey Hill

Jazz Piano Trios Minus You.........................MMO CD 6009
Jim Odrich, piano: Piano master Jim Odrich has compiled a great collection of classic jazz standards by the 20th century's greatest composers. Join the group here as Odrich performs his arrangements with the trio, then steps aside for you to work your own magic!
(I'm Getting) Sentimental over You; Satin Doll; Unforgettable; Someone to Light up My Life; Dream Dancing; Take the "A" Train; But Beautiful; Darn that Dream; I Had the Craziest Dream (from the film 'Hello, Frisco, Hello'): *I Had the Craziest Dream (from the film 'Hello, Frisco, Hello'); More than You Know*

The Jim Odrich Experience, with Orchestra ***Pop Piano Played Easy*** **..MMO CD 3062**
Jim Odrich, piano - various orchestras: Jim Odrich has created stunning piano-and-orchestra arrangements for these standards for piano with ensemble backgrounds. A real treat for pianists of all levels!
That's All; Misty; The Coffee Song; Fly Me to the Moon; The Girl from Ipanema; Triste; What Is This Thing Called Love?; If I Should Lose You; Prisoner of Love; All American: *Once Upon a Time*

Popular Piano Made Easy, with Orchestra ***Arranged by Jim Odrich*** .... **MMO CD 3063**
Jim Odrich, piano - various orchestras: Volume Two of Jim Odrich's two-part series of piano arrangements for a great collection of standards for piano with ensemble backgrounds.
All or Nothing at All; (Love Is) The Tender Trap; They Can't Take That Away from Me; Quiet Nights; Meditation; Wave; The Song Is You; I Hadn't Anyone 'Til You; Night and Day; Saturday Night (Is the Loneliest Night of the Week)

Studio Call: Film Scores (minus Piano) ...... **MMO CD 2071**
Tom Collier, Keyboards, Drums & Percussion; Howard Roberts, Guitar; Dan Dean, Electric Bass: *Main Title Theme; Nina's Love Theme; Search, The; Dancing with Cara; Chase, The; End Title*

Studio Call: Jazz/Fusion (minus Piano) .... **MMO CD 2081**
Tom Collier, Keyboards, Drums & Percussion; Howard Roberts, Guitar; Dan Dean, Electric Bass: *Padre's Dance; She's My Life; Tender Night; Black Hole; Ginger Snap*

Studio Call: Pop/Country (minus Piano) ...... **MMO CD 2096**
Tom Collier, Keyboards, Drums & Percussion; Howard Roberts, Guitar; Dan Dean, Electric Bass: *Alabama Lady; Another Rainy Night; Travelin' Willie; Reed between the Lines; Dolly's Day; Kenny's Gamble*

Studio Call: Rock/Funk (minus Piano) .... **MMO CD 2091**
Tom Collier, Keyboards, Drums & Percussion; Howard Roberts, Guitar; Dan Dean, Electric Bass: *Jackson Street; Hauling Oats; Toto Eclipse; Summer Work; Jar o' Funk*

Studio Call: Top 40 'MOR' (minus Piano) .... **MMO CD 2061**
Tom Collier, Keyboards, Drums & Percussion; Howard Roberts, Guitar; Dan Dean, Electric Bass:
Paul Didn't Say; All Day Long; Mindy; Make Your Move; The Way We Are; Dancing Girl

Studio City (minus Piano) .... **MMO CD 2025**
Cal State Northridge Jazz Ensemble: Studio City evolved as a response to the hundreds of requests over the years for MMO Big Band arrangements to play with. This entry features one of the foremost university bands in the nation, the Cal State, Northridge Jazz Ensemble, directed by Joel Leach. Listen to a pro soloist perform in the complete reference version with this outstanding group, then you step in so you can make your own impact! Features music from the pens of Sammy Nestico, Dave Leech, Mike Barone and more!
Dovie; Is There Anything Still There; The Opener; Big Dipper; Ladera Park; Word Was; Puesta del Sol; Northridge; Doin' Basie's Thing

Take One (minus Piano) .... **MMO CD 2015**
Jersey State College Jazz Ensemble/Dick Lowenthal: Dick Lowenthal's prize-winning ensemble, the Jersey Sate College Jazz Ensemble, is here presented performing the best of their book at the time these were recorded. ***2 CD Set***
She Cries; Snake Meets the Wizard; A Child Is Born; Dancing Men; Antithetical Arsis-Thesis; Nice n' Juicy; Blues for Ross

Sinatra Standards for Piano and Orchestra ***Arranged by Jim Odrich*** .... **MMO CD 3069**
Jim Odrich, piano - various orchestras: ver wonder what songs identified with Frank Sinatra would soundlike in the same arrangements, but with a piano substituted for the voice? Here are eleven such classics, arranged and performed by master pianist Jim Odrich. Listen to his renditions, then play them yourself with the exact transcriptions provided!
Come Rain or Come Shine; Witchcraft; The Best Is Yet to Come; This Is All I Ask; Meditation; Teach Me Tonight; It's All Right with Me; I've Got You Under My Skin; Young at Heart; It Might as Well Be Spring; All the Way

Stretchin' Out: ***'Comping' with a Jazz Rhythm Section*** .... **MMO CD 3060**
Wilber Ware, bass; George Duvivier, bass; Bobby Donaldson, drums; Ed Shaughnessy, drums: Two different Rhythm sections (bass & drums) accompany your playing of these blues and standards. Excellent practice in 'comping' (chording) styles in jazz.
Charleston Blues; Lullaby of the Leaves; Circle of Four Blues; Polka Dot Story; Cha-Cha; Foggy Baron; Low Down Blues; Waltz Time Blues; Medium Blues in G; Blues in the Night; April in Paris; Latin Scene; Porgy and Bess: *The Man I Love; Body and Soul; How About You?; Yancey Special; How High the Moon; Now's the Time*

Traditional Jazz Series ***The Condon Gang Adventures in New York & Chicago Jazz*** .... **MMO CD 6014**
Skjelbred, Ray, piano - Hal Smith's Rhythmakers: Bobby Gordon, clarinet; Chris Tyle, Trumpet; Clint Baker, trombone; Anita Thomas, tenor saxophone; Katie Cavera, guitar; Marty Eggers, bass; Hal Smith, leader and drums: From the 1920s to the 1950s, Eddie Condon and his band created a unique style of traditional jazz, characterized by a succession of instrumental solos and abrupt transitions of dynamics; the result reverberates to this day in the world of jazz. Now you can participate in this incredible style and the sophisticated music of the Condon Gang with this all-digital MMO release. Includes a stellar lineup of professionals giving you guidance and a fabulous ensemble with which to perform!
I Know that You Know; Strut Miss Lizzie; Jazz Me Blues; Skeleton Jangle; Monday Date; The One I Love Belongs to Somebody Else; A Kiss to Build a Dream on; I Must Have that Man; Georgia Grind

Student Series

The Art of Popular Piano Playing, vol. I ..... **MMO CD 3033**
Vinson Hill, piano: A guide to contemporary styles and techniques for any level of popular piano study. Read along and play along with your personal piano instructor, Vinson Hill. Discover the joy of learning how to arrange and perform old favorites and current songs in the modern idiom.
Introduction; Major Scales; Intervals; Cabin in the Sky; Triads & Chord Symbols; Three to Get Ready (Chord Rhythms & Arpeggios); A Preview; Six Chords: *The Sixth Story; More; What Is This Thing Called Love?; My Heart Stood Still; Around the World*

The Art Of Popular Piano Playing, vol. II .... **MMO CD 3034**
Vinson Hill, piano: This deluxe 2-CD set is the second in this 2-volume series. It contains the study of 7th chords, triads, and 7th chord inversions. In it Vinson Hill presents such style techniques as interval waltz bass, swing bass and arpeggio bass. ***2 CD Set***
Learn to Play; Birth of the Blues; Tea for Two; Someone to Watch over Me; Autumn Leaves; I Will Wait for You; Moon River; Mary Poppins: *Chim Chim Cheree*

'Pop' Piano For Starters (Student Level) .... **MMO CD 3035**
Vinson Hill, piano - Vinson Hill Quartet: Easy, swinging arrangements for listening and playing along. Vinson Hill, famous jazz pianist and teacher, shows you how it sounds. Then add your solo piano to the all-star rhythm section. Ideal for 2nd- and 3rd-year students. Eleven Standards plus YOU and the Vinson Hill Quartet!
Alfie; This Guy's in Love with You; What the World Needs Now (Is Love, Sweet Love); I Left My Heart in San Francisco; Sunny; Hello, Dolly!: *Hello, Dolly!; The Girl from Ipanema; Moon River; More (theme from 'Mondo Cane'); Love Is Blue;* Mary Poppins: *Chim Chim Cheree*

For our full catalogue of piano releases, visit us on the web at
www.musicminusone.com
50 Executive Blvd. • Elmsford, NY 10523
Call 1-800 669-7464 in the USA • 914 592-1188 International • Fax: 914 592-2751
email: info@musicminusone.com

MUSIC MINUS ONE
50 Executive Boulevard
Elmsford, New York 10523-1325
800-669-7464 (U.S.)/914-592-1188 (International)

www.musicminusone.com
e-mail: info@musicminusone.com

MMO 16011 Pub. No. 0943 Printed in Canada